SOCIAL STUDIES MATTERS!

WHAT IS GOVERNMENT?

PETER FINN

PowerKiDS press

Published in 2024 by The Rosen Publishing Group, Inc.
2544 Clinton Street, Buffalo, NY 14224

First Edition

Editor: Therese Shea
Book Design: Michael Flynn

Photo Credits: Cover Yaya Ernst/Shutterstock.com, p. 1; (series background) Eky Studio/Shutterstock.com; p. 5 Felipe Sanchez/Shutterstock.com; p. 7 Wileydoc/Shutterstock.com; p. 9 Aditya0635/Shutterstock.com; p. 11 Traceyaphotos2/Shutterstock.com; p. 13 LightField Studios/Shutterstock.com; p. 15 VectorMine/Shutterstock.com; p. 17 refrina/Shutterstock.com; p. 19 Mega Pixel/Shutterstock.com; p. 21 AVAVA/Shutterstock.com.

Library of Congress Cataloging-in-Publication Data

Names: Finn, Peter, 1978- author.
Title: What is government? / Peter Finn.
Description: Buffalo, New York : PowerKids Press, 2024. | Series: Social studies matters! | Includes index.
Identifiers: LCCN 2023036134 (print) | LCCN 2023036135 (ebook) | ISBN 9781499443950 (library binding) | ISBN 9781499443943 (paperback) | ISBN 9781499443967 (ebook)
Subjects: LCSH: Political science–United States–Juvenile literature. | United States–Politics and government–Juvenile literature.
Classification: LCC JA70 .F56 2024 (print) | LCC JA70 (ebook) | DDC 320.973–dc23/eng/20230809
LC record available at https://lccn.loc.gov/2023036134
LC ebook record available at https://lccn.loc.gov/2023036135

Manufactured in the United States of America

CPSIA Compliance Information: Batch #CWPK24. For Further Information contact Rosen Publishing at 1-800-237-9932.

CONTENTS

Laws and Government

Your family has rules. Your school has rules. Your government makes rules too. These rules are called laws. Laws keep people safe. A place's set of laws is a big part of its government. The government is also the people who make the laws and oversee the laws.

SPEED
LIMIT
30

Services

Governments do more than make laws. They **provide** services that people want and need. Parks, **libraries**, and schools are services. Police and fire **departments** are services too. Some governments also provide health care and food to those who need it.

FIRE STATION THREE
RALEIGH
CITY OF RALEIGH
3

Defense

Governments are also in charge of defending, or guarding, **citizens** from outside enemies. They have armed forces to do this. The army, navy, coast guard, **marines**, air force, and space force are the branches of the U.S. armed forces.

Kinds of Governments

Did you know there are different kinds of governments? Monarchies are governments headed by a monarch, or king or queen. Dictatorships are governments controlled by a ruler called a **dictator**. Democracies are governments run by citizens. The United States is a democracy. Canada is too.

Democracies

In a direct democracy, all citizens vote on government **decisions**. That would be hard to do in a big country! The United States and Canada are representative democracies. That means citizens **elect** people to represent, or act for, them in government.

VOTE

Three Branches

The U.S. national government is called the federal government. It's **divided** into three branches. The legislative branch makes the laws. The executive branch carries out the laws. The judicial branch explains the laws. The U.S. Constitution, the highest law, gives each branch its powers.

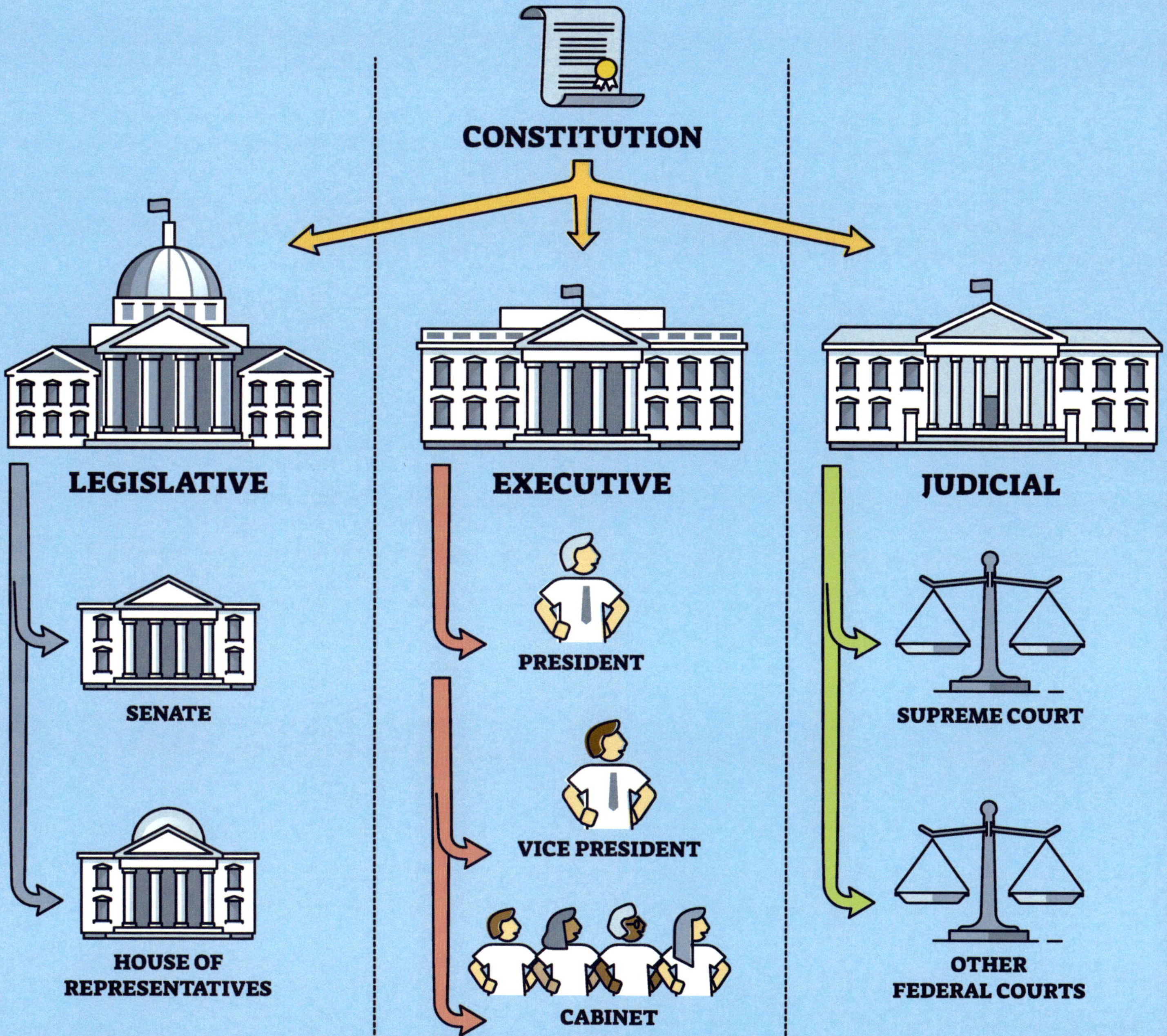
CONSTITUTION
LEGISLATIVE
EXECUTIVE
JUDICIAL
SENATE
HOUSE OF REPRESENTATIVES
PRESIDENT
VICE PRESIDENT
CABINET
SUPREME COURT
OTHER FEDERAL COURTS

Governments, Big and Small

The United States is a large country with many people. Its many communities have different needs. That's why there are different **levels** of government. States have governments. So do smaller communities, such as cities, towns, and villages. All have different laws and services.

CITY HALL

Taxes

A government needs money to do its work. It gets this money from taxes. Citizens pay different kinds of taxes to their governments. For example, you may pay tax on some things you buy. That's called sales tax.

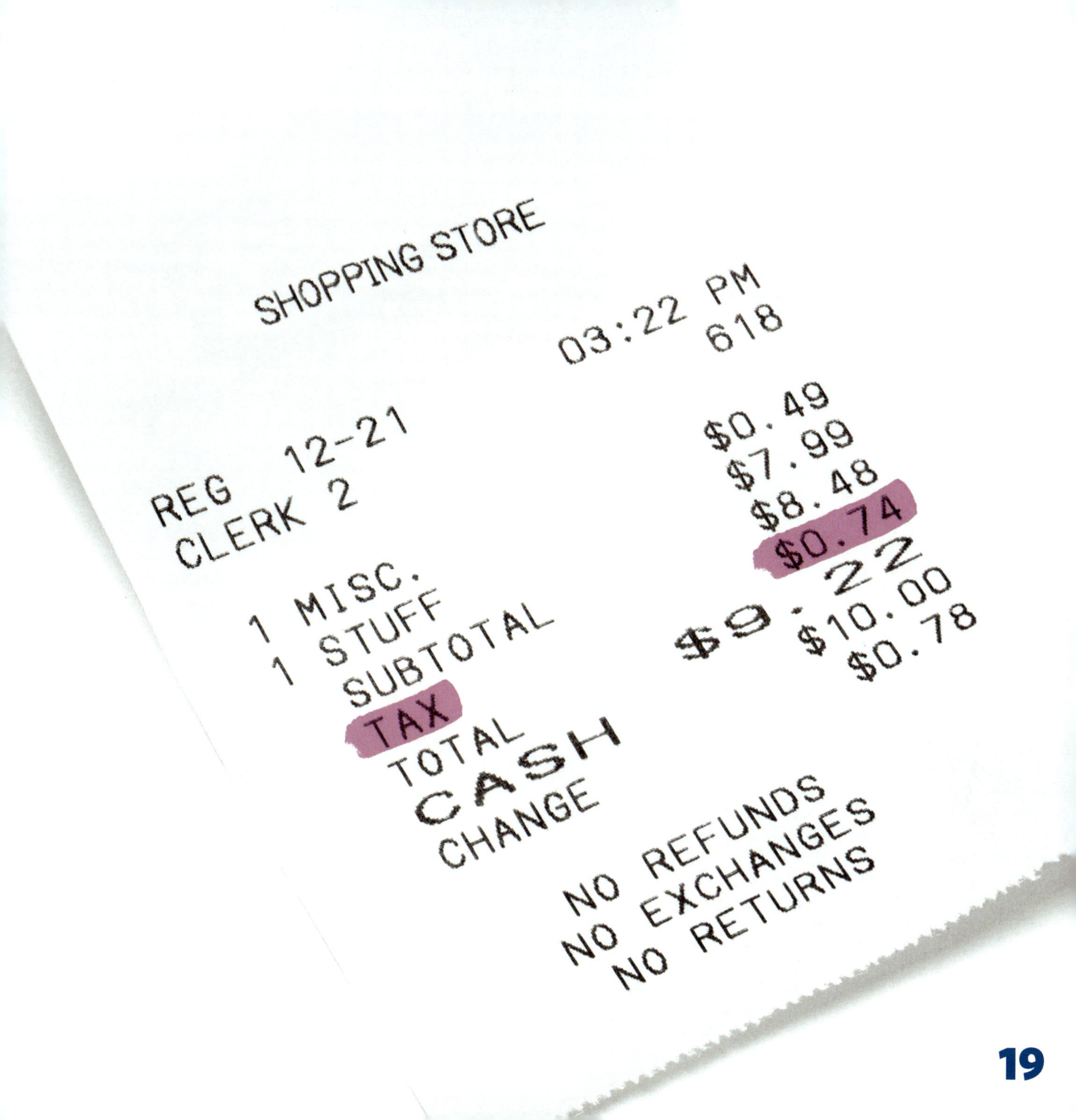
SHOPPING STORE
03:22 PM
618
REG 12-21
CLERK 2
1 MISC. $0.49
1 STUFF $7.99
SUBTOTAL $8.48
TAX $0.74
TOTAL $9.22
CASH $10.00
CHANGE $0.78
NO REFUNDS
NO EXCHANGES
NO RETURNS

It's *Your* Government

Governments make decisions that affect us all. Citizens in a democracy should take part in their government. If they can't be in the government, they should vote. If they can't vote yet, they can learn about their other rights. Get to know your government!

VOTE
VOTE
VOTE

GLOSSARY

citizen: Someone who lives in a country legally and has certain rights.

decision: A choice made after thinking about something.

department: A major part of a company, organization, government, or school.

dictator: Someone who rules a country by force.

divide: To break up.

elect: To choose for a position in a government.

level: A position or rank that is higher or lower when compared to other positions or ranks.

library: A place where books are kept.

marine: A soldier who serves at sea and on land.

provide: To supply for use.

FOR MORE INFORMATION

BOOKS

Foster, Jeff. *For Which We Stand: How Our Government Works and Why It Matters*. New York, NY: Scholastic Inc., 2020.

Winn, Kevin P. *How Do the Three Branches of Government Work Together?* Ann Arbor, MI: Cherry Lake Publishing, 2023.

WEBSITES

Ben's Guide to the U.S. Government
bensguide.gpo.gov/
Check out this fun guide to the U.S. government.

United States Government for Kids
www.ducksters.com/history/us_government.php
Find links to what you want to know about the government.

Publisher's note to educators and parents: Our editors have carefully reviewed these websites to ensure that they are suitable for students. Many websites change frequently, however, and we cannot guarantee that a site's future contents will continue to meet our high standards of quality and educational value. Be advised that students should be closely supervised whenever they access the internet.

INDEX